Plainsongs

Editor

Eric R. Tucker

Associate Editors

Becky Faber, Michael Catherwood,
Eleanor Reeds, Ali Beheler

Publisher

Patricia Oman, HC Press

Production Assistant

Jenny Sells

Cover art by Chris Goedert

Hastings College Press | Hastings, Nebraska
https://www.hastings.edu/hastings-college-press/

Subscriptions to *Plainsongs* are $20.00 annually for two issues, published in January and July.

Plainsongs welcomes submissions. The manuscript deadline for the Fall/Winter 2020/21 issue is June 15, 2020. Contributors will receive one free copy of the issue in which their poem appears.

Please use our online submission manager, available on our website, to submit work. Though we will endeavor to consider both e-mailed and snail-mailed submissions, these are not our preferred submission methods and we cannot guarantee responses for such submissions. All other correspondence can be e-mailed to the editor at plainsongs@hastings.edu or addressed to the editor at

> *Plainsongs*
> Hastings College Press
> 710 N. Turner Ave.
> Hastings, NE 68901

Plainsongs is indexed by Humanities International Complete, EBSCO Information Services, 10 Estes Street, Ipswich, MA 01938.

ISBN-13 978-1-942885-73-3

ISSN 1534-3820

Plainsongs

Winner of the Jane Geske Award,
presented by the Nebraska Center for the Book

Notes from the Editor

With this issue, *Plainsongs* turns forty, and, unlike its current editor, who only vaguely recalls what that felt like, it is showing no sign of a post-thirties hangover, none of the hallmarks of an impending/ongoing midlife crisis, no evidence of rapidly encroaching decrepitude. Who knows? Maybe it really is true that life begins at forty. Of course, in geologic time, all of us were practically born yesterday. In lit journal years, though, *Plainsongs* is undeniably an old-timer: since its inception in 1980, countless artfully made, well-meaning, high-minded print journals and magazines have come and gone. *Plainsongs*, however, has managed to defy the long odds and overcome the obstacles—time, cost, online competition, shrinking subscriber base, etc.—such publications face. After all these years, *Plainsongs* is still here, still alive, still kicking, still enjoying the 80s-era musical stylings of Simple Minds. Its longevity is largely due to the efforts of former editors Dwight Marsh and Laura Marvel-Wunderlich, who, through their expert stewardship, put *Plainsongs* in a position to thrive for many years to come. We hope to be around another ten years, another twenty years, even longer. Will you still need *Plainsongs*, and will you still feed *Plainsongs*, when it is sixty-four? *Plainsongs* certainly hopes so.

So how will *Plainsongs* celebrate its fortieth birthday? *Plainsongs* would prefer not to make a huge fuss. It's not even sure it feels like going out tonight; its favorite chair is right over there. But you are all invited to the soiree. In this fortieth-anniversary issue you will find *Plainsongs*' three Winter 2020 award poems—"Winter," by Miriam Jacobs; "The Daily Tragedy," by Kate Polak; and "Grandfather's Hands," by Nathan Manley—along with award essays by our fabulous associate editors Becky Faber, Eleanor Reeds, and Michael Catherwood. Featuring beautiful cover art by Chris Goedert, this issue resonates with vibrant, vital songs composed by talented poets from around the world.

Forty is a milestone: for pop songs, for people, for poetry journals. As John Lennon wrote in his 1980 song "(Just Like) Starting Over," "Our life together / Is so precious together. / We have grown, we have grown. / Although our love still is special / Let's take a chance and fly away somewhere." We hope you'll keep taking a chance on us. Come on in. It'll be just like starting over.

Eric R. Tucker, editor

Contents

Winter 10
    Miriam Jacobs
About "Winter":
A *Plainsongs* Award Poem 11
    Becky Faber
The Daily Tragedy 12
    Kate Polak
About "The Daily Tragedy":
A *Plainsongs* Award Poem 13
    Eleanor Reeds
Grandfather's Hands 14
    Nathan Manley
About "Grandfather's Hands":
A *Plainsongs* Award Poem 15
    Michael Catherwood
The Book of Broken Things 16
    Glenn Freeman
Appassionata 17
    David Capps
Dining Out 18
    Elizabeth Landrum
All Things Unpleasant 19
    Mark Sanders
In Winter 20
    Alison Hicks
Self-Portrait with a Box of Brownies 21
    Yvonne Higgins Leach
Easter Dress 22
    Alfred Fournier
Sundowning 23
    Chase Dimock
Flotsam & History 24
    Mark B. Hamilton
Behind Door 14 25
    Carl Boon
On Seeing Many Ants in the Kitchen 26
    Wesley Sexton
Ellipses 28
    S. B. Merrow
Apology 29
    Beth Paulson
"Salad Days" 30
    Erika Donald
Struggling to Retain Her Memory 32
    Mark Thalman

To My Father's Ashes 33
    Steven M. Smith
Cain 34
    Annyston H. Pennington
Dear Mr. Stevens 36
    Mark Robinson
At the Corner of New Orleans and Frontier, Disneyland 37
    Matt Mason
Blue Decisions 38
    Daniel Edward Moore
Your Room 39
    Elise Hempel
Birds 40
    Randel McCraw Helms
The Bigger Person 41
    Anastasia Jill
March 42
    Daisy Bassen
Hard and Sharp 43
    D.S. Maolalai
On Becoming a Harp 44
    Joy S. Mahar
To Be Daphne 46
    Kristina Heflin
The Fox 47
    Christian Woodard
Telephone of the Wind 48
    Suzanne O'Connell
What You Hold at Bay 49
    Pam Baggett
On Her Blindness 50
    Phillip Howerton
Coming Down in Changzhou 51
    James A. Miller
The Mist Blower 52
    Eleanor Reeds
will no one love you Margaret 53
    Emily Ellison
Adulthood 54
    Diana Donovan
pawnee poem 55
    Henry Krusiewicz
Attendance 56
    Max Heinegg
Describe the Rain as Dishwater 57
    Deborah H. Doolittle
The Old Woman Thinks the Doll Alive 58
    Vicki Mandell-King

The Man Who Worked for Me 59
 James Longstaff
Sun splashed rye grass, near rose perfume in the garden 60
 Libby Bernardin
Of Snow 61
 Mary Ann Meade
June, ... 62
 Calida Osti
Melancholy 64
 Roxanne Prillwitz
Local Giraffe 65
 Kenneth Pobo
Trespass 66
 Mark Metcalf
The Poet Parents 67
 Charissa Menefee
Walking on Broughton & Hillsborough 68
 Patricia Lauren Ndombe
Into the Woods 69
 Jennifer Brown
Angel of Repose 70
 Angelika Quirk
Burial 72
 Olivia Swasey
Barnacle 73
 Casey Lynn Roland
Notes from the Dragon's Autopsy 74
 Scott Thomas Lumbard
Objects of Shame 75
 Alyssa Ross
The Least I Can Do 76
 Becky Faber
At the carne asada 77
 Gabriel Mundo
The War Started. A Cartoon 78
 Thomas Mixon
A Ballad of Anchors & Scythes 79
 George Looney
Lights Out 80
 Jen Schneider
Night Light 82
 E. R. Lutken
dead language 83
 Debora Ewing
Yeghegnadzor: Arid Orange 84
 Alex Vartan Gubbins
Ode to a Centipede 85
 Gloria Heffernan

Why Are All of the White Babies at the Deep End of the Swimming Pool? 86
    Monica Weatherly
Once Upon a Time, There Were Two Girls..88
    Stacey Balkun
Running from December 90
    Brett Thompson
Firewood 91
    Dave Malone
How to Pan for Gold..92
    Ronnie Sirmans
The Mask 93
    P M F Johnson
Something to Write Home About 94
    Michael Malan
Volcano 95
    Celia Meade
Hard-bitten Body 96
    Andrea Fry
Surrender 97
    Victor Altshul
Dry 98
    Monty Jones
Moving Day 99
    Claudia Buckholts
The Coffee Table 100
    Georgette Unis
Phone Conversations with an Outdated Insurance Claim................................101
    Devon Clements
Pulling Down the Peach Tree, 1964..102
    Michael Catherwood
I Write to You..103
    Evalyn Lee
Chamoy Lollypop 104
    Katherine Hoerth
A Knack for Folding Things 105
    Kathleen Corcoran
Goodbye Earth, ...106
    Melissa Sanders
Cycle of Nature 107
    Marc Swan
Paper Lips 108
    Sara Lynn Burnett
My Traveling Heart 109
    Barbara Ryder-Levinson
her heart upon her sleeve for daws to peck at..110
    Maya Chhabra

Winter

At first, the flecks are few,
with almost a minute between sightings,
not really what you might call *snow*,
but before you arrange this thought into sentences,
it's coming down thicker,
particles so ashy and weightless
you wonder how they can land,
although you knew it would come to this:
you are alone
and it's snowing words that fail you;
turn a knob—it's agony;
stairs hurt your knees;
you stand weeping in the kitchen
over a cork you can't dislodge; soon
the family will wonder more often,
louder, about winter's slow assembly and removal,
persuade you with their exhausted faces
to a thick decline:
you will let your heels dry,
stop waxing your upper lip,
give up the organic bit,
forget to secret your wishes under cover of dark,
pretend not to see *No Smoking*.
She always did use *the situation*, they'll say—

Miriam Jacobs
Atlanta, Georgia

About "Winter":
A *Plainsongs* Award Poem

As soon as I finished reading "Winter" for the first time, I went back to re-read it aloud. The fluency of the lines is impressive, making it especially easy to read aloud.

I was taken by how effectively the poet uses the metaphor of falling snow with the aging process, a place where "it's snowing words that fail you...." This type of nature/aging comparison is common, but it is generally not as well done as in "Winter." The parallel of falling snow with diminishing abilities is strongly developed. In each case, the actual occurrence comes without language, "although you knew it would come to this." It was at this line that I pulled out an anthology to find Robert Frost's "Nothing Gold Can Stay" where he writes, "So dawn goes down to day. / Nothing gold can stay."

"Winter" explores the specifics of the loss of one's golden period—the agony of trying to turn a knob, the way knees hurt when climbing stairs, the frustration of trying to remove a cork from a bottle. The synthesis of these situations is nicely portrayed by the line "...winter's slow assembly and removal" and lead a person to "forget to secret your wishes under cover of dark"—which I think is the saddest line of the poem.

The generational chasm explored in the poem reminds us of Frost's warning that "Nature's first green is gold, / Her hardest hue to hold. / Her early leaf's a flower; / But only so an hour." "Winter" may not be a comforting poem, but it is a true one.

Becky Faber
Lincoln, Nebraska

The Daily Tragedy

for Anita Hill, Christine Blasey Ford, and the rest of us.

It is a hill. The climb is steep, you slip
where no one wants to catch you. You are the hill,
you are a crest that's—through its topography—
meant to be conquered. You are a metaphor.

It is a river. It must be crossed, but
to ford it, you lose something: your shoe, your name,
the sense stories give you: that all will right
in the end. You will be across, which makes

the fording "worth it." You don't yet know how
the wilderness works. There is no top or base,
no end across the water—the river is
better likening, but only shat in upstream.

Unknowingly, you wade into the clear water,
but it sticks to you. It sticks.

Kate Polak
Yellow Springs, Ohio

About "The Daily Tragedy":
A *Plainsongs* Award Poem

The title of this sonnet and its dedication not only to the women who testified against two of our current Supreme Court Justices but to "the rest of us" emphasize the ubiquity of the experiences described, a ubiquity that justifies the universality of Kate Polak's second-person address. The "Me Too" movement has built power through consciousness raising, enabling women to speak out about their suffering and to demand that such gender-based violence be recognized as a structural phenomenon. "The Daily Tragedy" reveals the isolation of individual women: the only reference to potential companionship and assistance during the heroine's frustrating journey is to "no one."

Polak's use of the present tense and tersely declarative statements such as "It must" and "You will" enforce the reader's participation in the thankless task of testimony, of being and reclaiming what Sara Ahmed terms a "feminist killjoy." The performative power of language is reserved for the privileged. The names bestowed upon Anita Hill and Christine Blasey Ford by patriarchal conventions become their destinies. The poet is able to make us all into metaphors while we can only lose our names and "the sense stories give you." The punning use of Hill and Ford's names also indicates the bitter humor of this sonnet, which demands to be spat out in a sarcastic tone, most especially through its ironic vocalization of "worth it." ("It" is not and, *contra* L'Oréal, neither are you.) The sonic landscape of the poem is populated by the harsh "c" and the hissing "s" as well as the glide of "w" that the former sounds besmirch in the sonnet's closing image.

The persistence required for bearing witness is literalized by Polak's terrain, which is difficult to navigate and constantly retards progress. Every line in the sonnet is punctuated by at least one caesura as Polak approximates blank verse while also disrupting its apparently natural flow with relentless monosyllables. The final line of the poem is left incomplete as the resolution of an ending is withheld from the reader: "you" are left stranded in a stream, shit sticking to your legs and unable to move forward. Time cannot be up quickly enough.

Eleanor Reeds
Hastings, Nebraska

Grandfather's Hands

Archimedean, his affinity
for machines: an attic fan's old complaint
still groans through the empty space of him—
ancient farmhouse hollow. *How different
it might have been,* my mother repeated
in her plaintive recollections as she picked
through tatters of earth-worn mythologies:
his workshop's arch, a cathedral of rust;
in the scrape and hiss of the lathe, clangor
as of bells; gardens of scrap iron and
the pearled octaves of his accordion
over masterless arcane mechanisms.
    Your hands, she used to say, *just like his hands—*
mine, that bleed only in winter, unstung
by work, fleshy, white, and soft as a page,
uncalloused, shaped by these finer engines.

Nathan Manley
Loveland, Colorado

About "Grandfather's Hands": A *Plainsongs* Award Poem

In Nathan Manley's fine-tuned poem on his "Grandfather's Hands," we enjoy a tight and rich journey that bears down on the elemental mechanisms of time, a life told through details, and a grandfather's "affinity / for machines."

Manley balances details between solid mechanical things and the emotions of loss as he develops these narratives organically in the poem. Sounds of the items are often depicted: the "clangor / ... of bells" along with the "scrape and hiss of the lathe." The grandfather's story is never lost to emotion and often surprising images are presented. The poet writes about a "fan" that "still groans through the empty space of him." Manley employs objects to help illustrate the character of the man: a "lathe," "scrap iron," and an "accordion." These possessions document that the grandfather is longed for and missed.

Manley executes the metaphors in the poem with the same precision as a machine: "attic fan's old complaint"; "cathedral of rust"; and "gardens of scrap iron." These striking images bring great depth and beauty to the poem, creating a unique fullness to the grandfather's personal character.

The poem's turn at the end is forceful in its understatement. The interjection of speech, "*Your hands... just like his hands—*" brings the reader back to the poem's title, and we see the speaker's hands "that bleed only in winter," hands "soft as a page," hands "shaped by these finer engines."

A poem can be a miraculous fine engine itself, taking us far off in time then bringing us back, all in 16 lines.

Michael Catherwood
Omaha, Nebraska

The Book of Broken Things

How we live
on the edge
of a shoe about
to drop. The lightbulb pops
into blackness; the gate's
hanging on one hinge.
The tire's flat, the mower
won't start, the penis
won't rise—we're talking
metaphor baby, allegory.
The bulldozer sits
motionless spewing smoke
in a pool of mud. In
his last years, Paul Klee's
body had almost frozen
in place, each movement
more painful than the last.
Yet still he kept painting
his angels, artistic
transformation itself
a symptom. Not sure
if it's the diagnosis
or a compensatory human
response. I'm no doctor.
But I do know
when things are broken.
We are beautiful; it's natural
to have our hearts
broken. We will be
forgiven our grandiose
beauty and all
we never quite complete.

Glenn Freeman
Mount Vernon, Iowa

Appassionata

A bird alight a phoenix stone. Iterations
of words. Allegro assai across a headstone,
faded squall of tail feather, forefinger trilling
white keys, appassionata sonata. Wants

the stone sculpture to be a fountain, wants
to be a bird, to have a small reflection cross
the water, a warmth to erupt through snow.
Lines inscribed on gravestones, emboldened

by her small clawing, her miscellaneous
fluttering which makes certain names appear
and reappear. Bird in greek was palm for phoenix,
phoenix in greek was palm for bird, palm

in greek, phoenix for bird, phrases scratch away,
phrases in phrasis, atavisms on brownstone,
atoms in tightly packed stone planes, molecular
condensations, condescensions, engines of false

spring, as if so much had gone into my attempt
to make sense of it, but not enough.

David Capps
New Haven, Connecticut

Dining Out

So many want to know
how we are this evening,
if we'd like to leave
our coats at the door, or drape them
over the backs of our chairs,
if we'd like lemon slices in our water,
how rare you prefer your filet, and
if tonight I will take my salad dressed
or naked, vinaigrette on the side.

But what I want to know is how many
more times we'll be sitting here
or there, our wine glasses filled again
and again with empty conversations,
pretending to care about each other
more than the tang of the hollandaise,
tonight's surly server, or words overheard
from the neighboring table.

Today, after I checked our calendar
for conflicts, I watched myself place
the red beret above one eyebrow
as you looped your best striped tie
like always, polished your shoes
with a lick of your fingers, cracked each
knuckle twice. I could smell the smolder
from the night before. We did not speak

until the air was so frozen and thick
it had to be broken. This time you held
the ice pick. You asked which restaurant
I'd chosen. *The same as last time*
I said, because I did not want to
consider an alternative.

Elizabeth Landrum
Lopez Island, Washington

All Things Unpleasant

lie beneath the bed, boxed up and banded,
mementos, like baseball cards—Willie Mays or Roberto Clemente;
like rocks—agates and fossils, arrowheads and flint scrapers—
lifted from old creek beds where old reunions
approximate the clutter, chatter, and chill
we dwell on. These are the boogey men.
These are neighborhoods into which we turned
and forgot ourselves, photographs coated with measurable dust:
sisters and friends, dead or, because we do not talk,
distance a map invalidated and the way here eradicated,
shut behind doors of place and posture and forgetfulness.
They are old lovers, old lovers, old lovers
whose touch or kiss or smell compels though petals in the box
darken. All kept, news reports or letters or report cards, an archive
sad and longingly beautiful, beautiful being that cheap but true
    word.

It's how we became heroic, the accumulated embarrassments
of best times, horrible as they were, that make us wealthy.
We put them away but call them forward,
evoke and provoke them. Demons and angels,
ghosts that tap the bed's footboard,
let me share you with those I still love or wish to love.
I wish to love everyone. Welcome to my house,
clapped together of shingles and sheetrock salvaged
from pride and angst, the dumping ground is such a market!
We may have collections that are complementary. I wish to trade—
See here the drum sticks that beat my heart.
See here the lock of hair of the one who fled the world.
See here, see here, the expensive watch whose hand stands still
so we may have this moment together and never leave.

Mark Sanders
Nacogdoches, Texas

In Winter

After the college tour,
my son asks what it's like in winter.
We are looking out over Lake Champlain,
in short sleeves, having eaten lunch in a repurposed garage,
bay doors rolled up to let the outdoors in.
Long, my husband and I say at the same time.
There's a lot of snow, we say, though we know he knows that
much, and in any case, no place gets the snowfalls
of our childhood anymore.
It snows in May, my husband says, *but it melts pretty fast.*

Across the water—impossible that this could freeze,
dark blue and untroubled as clarified sky—
a sightseeing boat decked in party lights
moves steadily toward us.
How to transmit the knowledge
we grew up with and he did not?
To tell the truth, we've gotten used
to where we are living now,
and the memory dims within us.

Pressing the brake impertinently,
radio blaring into the drift,
I slide across the whitened road
so slowly it seems to take seventeen years.

Alison Hicks
Havertown, Pennsylvania

Self-Portrait with a Box of Brownies

I would have liked to bake
with my mother.
But there were six of us
and she had laundry to fold
groceries to buy, bills to pay
beds to change, floors to scrub
meals to make and animals to feed.
Baking was a luxury.
By the time I was old enough
to stir cookie dough, the world
capitalized further and everything
became precut, precooked
prepackaged and preprocessed.
Still, I would have loved to bake
brownies even from a box with her.
She went to work
when I was eleven
and never looked back.

Yvonne Higgins Leach
Vashon, Washington

Easter Dress

Mom died and then wore green,
as if spring held her breath.

As if her seedpod casket,
shallow in desolate earth,
might burst into flower
with the first warm rain.

As if her eyes could smile,
struck by a rainbow of tulips
planted as lifeless bulbs,
soil beneath her nails.

As if blooming and gay
among sisters and cousins
she could hear them plead,
Francis, what is your secret?

Then plead again, at the service
where her green dress
surpassed lilies   propped
stiff and white beside her.

Alfred Fournier
Phoenix, Arizona

Sundowning

At sundown she cannot find
the Christmas presents in the oven.
She sprinkles fish food on the television
wonders when President Reagan
will bring those hostages home.

Hence, I am late to the restaurant
and he's always understanding
always holds my hand across
the table, looks into my eyes
first with empathy, then a squint
trying to detect a mutating gene
a faint skip in the neurons firing

He orders me a double bourbon
two more by the end of the night
says he wants me to loosen up
forget about nurses and Medicare
but as I stumble to the door
drop my keys in the planter
and slur a sorry, I know his arm
around mine is a test run.

Chase Dimock
Studio City, California

Flotsam & History

Caught in the song
I hurry beneath a hammock of power lines
stretched river-wide at the Crain Brothers dock
defined by a fast current from the storm in upstate
New York and by the squirrels swimming in a furry
bridge remembered from a history book.

A signal light flashes Red, Yellow, then Green,
dropping me down into a concrete box of the lock,
the walls speckled with bugs and water fleas—a cascade
aglow with wasps and spider webs.

I am the idle caretaker lulled by soft sounds
sinking into shade with the dory nudging the gray grit
and snugging at the end of its line.

I row in rhythms through flotsam,
through chucks of wood and Styrofoam cups
into the mist drifting down from the churning
water in the rocks at the foot of the dam,
a falling froth of trees, pointed, broken-off limbs
spinning in an apparition of orange flesh peeled back
like a fish held sideways in a snake's mouth.

And then the long span of Pennsylvania Power,
the salvage yards and towboat terminals,
and the roots tangling out from steep banks of sand islands
where I stop beneath the maples that hide bird songs
along a river widening into everywhere.

Nothing is wasted. Nothing is denied.
Even the space between heartbeats becomes a pause
where everything just stops, picks up,
and moves on.

Mark B. Hamilton
Dunedin, Florida

Behind Door 14

My grandmother uncrosses her legs
and crosses them again. She's holding
a pigeon, a boy's hand

not mine though she calls it mine
and the air is full of Christmas
and the scent of afghans
and presents nobody has the nerve

to open. It's possible that nothing can be
opened here; it's possible I've moved
too quickly and pushed

the wrong door. This is a fragile place
where nothing fits, where holy things
collide with things gone wrong.
Her face is not the face I knew,

and look how slim she is,
how vigilant the corners of her mouth,
and the window's cracked.

It must have been some boy
had thrown a baseball high, some boy
she'd mistaken for me. But I am here,
I didn't do it, I'm mostly happy,

I swear. If Shalimar perfume
could fill the room that's not a room…
if she'd only hold a glass of ice-water

with a strand of lemon, then I could know
I haven't come too soon, that perhaps
I missed a door that hid
my old familiarity.

Carl Boon
Barberton, Ohio

On Seeing Many Ants in the Kitchen

And instead of crunching these tiny
eyelashes between my thumb
and forefinger, I delight in how many
little lives my excesses can sustain
on a Tuesday like this one. One
sidewalk splash, for example,
of my peanut-butter ice cream can
keep a dozen bees licking their chops
for a good half hour, and if the crumbs
idling in the corners of my cabinets
attract the interest of every bug
in the neighborhood, sending them
marching in a line to my backdoor,
I can play the generous host for a while.
Why begrudge them, my fellow
scavengers? For haven't I more than once
feasted on the unwanted delicacies
my friends left behind, snatching
K's half-gone pancake from a
stack of bussed dishes or brushing
the grass off M's still-meaty
apple core or wiping, with some bread,
the bottom of A's soup bowl?
Besides, no matter how I wash
my hands or scrub the kitchen floor,
the dirt will always reach for me.
Death will go about in his patched
overalls like some filthy farmer,
turning his giant and mud-mangled
heaps, adding new to old, mixing
uniformly all that once was and
spooning it by the spadeful to all
that is hungry and might yet be.
Eventually, my body will smorgasbord
whole villages of sleep-starved
microbes working overtime to
make the earth fertile and loamy.
Communities of rind-drunk fruitfly

and larvaworm will buzz with repurposed
electricity. The thought fills me
with a terrible joy. It sends my heart
skittering into the corners of my chest
like some pink-red and hungry bug.

Wesley Sexton
Greensboro, North Carolina

Ellipses

When no means *no*
until it means *yes*,
words are sacrifice,
tongues for the starving,
bright sour things
to suck in gratitude,
offered in minor keys
that mock the moment

Nothing is clear

except its opposite—
voices of *miel* sticky as facts
and true so rarely you ask
why now and in what language?

But there they lie

like light on the sheet,
airy and entering
lands you've never seen,
and before you can cry
no! not this . . .
they sing you back
with animal songs,
your first memories
of the naked choir.

S. B. Merrow
Baltimore, Maryland

Apology

Please forgive me for taking
the persimmons from your old tree—
they were the high ones hanging
up against the blue sky where only
the birds could get to them.
I used the long-handled crook
I found in your open garage
to reach and free each bright fruit
from the branch that held it tight
so it would fall onto the grass below.

Around the stem of one I cut a circle,
lifted out the soft core, then spooned
the ripe sweet fruit into my mouth,
even scraped the bits that clung
inside its slick skin. It tasted
both honeyed and tart, like love.

Each globe I held in my hands
was a heart of red-orange, a scrap
of saffron silk, a tanager's breast.
You weren't home when I looked in
your back window and saw on a chair
just inside the door a basket full of suns.

Beth Paulson
Ouray, Colorado

"Salad Days"

There are days when I just want
to eat a chunk of pie
at the sink
in underpants
crumbs tumbling
not worrying
about ants.
Some days
I don't run
I don't do
anything good.
I drive three blocks
my face
my hair
unwashed
for a salami sandwich
and I'm a vegetarian.
I'll eat it outside
on the deck
with a beer
a cold glass.
I'll let the cats
wander out
stretch
sniff the air
absorb the heat
like inmates
released.
There is so much
to worry about
the fleas
pesticides.
It will eat up
your insides.
They slip
through the slats
drop down
to the grass.

I get a spoon
a pint of mint chip.

**Erika Donald
Berkeley, California**

Struggling to Retain Her Memory

Mom writes notes to herself
and keeps them on the kitchen counter.
She studies each one like a scholar
trying to discover a great mystery.

Turn off stove. Brush teeth. Get mail.

Afraid to answer the door, she ignores the bell,
knowing she can't recall if the face
is a stranger or friend. Once again,
she gazes at herself in the mirror
and doesn't see the need to use a comb.

Yesterday, my aunt phoned, "Your father—
perforated ulcer, come quick!"

So far into denial, Dad didn't dial 911
for an ambulance. Instead,
he loaded himself into their Chevy Impala
and gave Mom directions to the hospital.
If he had passed out, she would have been found
driving aimlessly around—
lost in a storm of blaring horns
with a dead man in the back seat.

Mark Thalman
Forest Grove, Oregon

To My Father's Ashes

If I had my forgiving way to give
My father breath again and press my fear
To his relentless cold—let him relive
A moment much like the unstable beer

Bottle he raised the day in May I came
Into this world of his—I would not love
The grief he raised nor the relentless shame
I tried to bury under his heap of

Bad luck, blunders, and binges. So I took my
Forgiving way and carried his ashes
Along the boyhood path to my hiding
Spot in the sheltered woods where shade flashes

Between the ferns that fence my bed of moss.
And there I knelt and then tucked in my loss.

Steven M. Smith
North Syracuse, New York

Cain

to wash your hands in dogblood

to shut a door
     with tenderness

to gaze down at a bird flattened in the alley and think it a pressed
    flower

toeing through the world with an eye for cruelty

for beauty and the thread of spit
which links their mouths

I have long since feared a painful death
though nothing comes

in the wheatfield gold and hollowed
my brother stands with his

back to me   come
back to me

     to cross the distance of selves   by knife blade

to bask in the thunder of your name thrown
        down the sky's vault

to bleed the lamb

to share fruit with bare hands

pulp collecting beneath the gray crescent of
a thumb nail

to suck clean

trying to reach you   across the black ravine
            of time

how I call your name and the echo throws back mine

Annyston H. Pennington
Amarillo, Texas

Dear Mr. Stevens

Here the birds sound like howling dogs
in the middle of the day
in the middle of the desert.
At night words like *feather* and *fluttering*
fill my dreams.
There is something harsh
about the front lawns of pebbles and sand
but the pale moon hangs large over downtown
in constant morning sun.
The pastel yellow plaster of the Roman church,
its beautifully manicured and deep green grass
stands out as the sort of haven
you would have searched out in this dusty town.
I imagine alone in the darkness, in a pew
among the candles and the crucifix,
your face still and your eyes closed
wrestling to reconcile the real with the imagined
arranging, deepening, enchanting
never hearing the pounding on the door,
the crowd of us frantic to get in.

Mark Robinson
West Des Moines, Iowa

At the Corner of New Orleans and Frontier, Disneyland

Under Old West guitar and Jazz band trumpet,
where the riverboat steam horn blares,
you order a corn dog.

Beignets and étouffée
are down the way, cowboy,
you don't have to put up with that.

But the sun dips into everybody's eyes,
strollers full of screams rock by
and you

start searching, at the popcorn cart and in your life,
for something more
than everything

you've been settling
for.

Matt Mason
Omaha, Nebraska

Blue Decisions

If obedience means fear can be learned
        easily in the dark at home
                after heaven does something awful

like polish the buckle with moon & stars
        & before the earth does something worse
                like shred the skin with its mouth of gravel

bleeding on roads of a childhood lost
        somewhere between waist & knees
                that virginal vortex of violence praised

for history blacking out in my mouth
        for tomorrow weeping not for me, but for all
                blue decisions still unmade,

those sperm shaped eggs
        in a carton cracked
                in the corner like you & me.

Daniel Edward Moore
Oak Harbor, Washington

Your Room

No sign now with your name that says it's yours
embellished with a penguin, purple flowers

or framed by peace signs, when you were a teen,
as though you welcomed me. No need to lean

in and listen at the lock before
I tap and tell you time for bed or supper,

to tiptoe past closed conferences with friends.
I can walk right in now, I can stand

inside your empty closet, boldly stroll
across the space where your queen bed once ruled.

No sign now with your name and its firm
apostrophe and "s," just this open

door all mine, this quiet as I scrape
away the stubborn ghosts of Scotch tape.

Elise Hempel
Charleston, Illinois

Birds

"A poem should always have birds in it,"
Said Mary Oliver, even if it's just
Vultures, lice-filled, drifting down naked-necked
Toward a thing maggoted and softly swelling.

There, you may approach, oblique, downwind;
The quarry is shy. Set aside what you've been told,
What they do is cleansing, sacred, reducing
Merest carrion to enriching soil of dung.

Or else watch, if you must, white, nesting swans
Delight among reeds, mid-river, safely islanded,
Downy cygnets soon to come. But why, I ask,
Do you think these the more beautiful?

Randel McCraw Helms
Fountain Hills, Arizona

The Bigger Person

I grow into my enemies—
like combat boots; toy soldiers, plastic boys, a model gun—
the perfect weapon for me,
the soldier girl
versus men
who want to
tear my
rosebud.

Anastasia Jill
Orlando, Florida

March

On St. Patrick's Day, reading Irish poetry
Before bed, it could be a tradition,
A private one that you'd only share
With someone who knows the difference
Between Counties, how one river curls
Through a city and another crawls, oiled
On its surface, inked into the earth, cream
Unskimmed, separate.

        It isn't green here,
Not yet, not at all. We tried to let the children
Run on the field, still sere, olivine, crusts
Of snow worth kicking. We brought them in
Early, we held their cold hands. Unlucky
To be so cold when the sky was so blue,
The light teasing, the coquetry of primavera,
Libertines at play. I read about Colette today,
How there were no snakes to be cast out
Of Eire, *le blé en herbe*, the love affair begun
With a youth. The blurring of rouge
On the thinning mouth of a matron;

        I read about
Green, betrayal, the parade time takes us on,
The snakeskin left in the unmown grass.
The children ran, clamored to come inside,
Already familiar with disappointment, wise
Enough to wait for better weather.

Daisy Bassen
East Greenwich, Rhode Island

Hard and Sharp

she came back from india
with gifts for the family,
with a new tattoo,
and without the girlfriend
she had taken over there. carefully
I didn't ask
what happened
because I find you can't
just ask these things—said other things
instead
and asked her about india,
and about vietnam and her time in tibet. my sister
is hard, sharp and cynical
and very funny—she went to those places
not to discover herself
at the feet of some swami
or to learn
anything about them
but just
because it beat working
here another year. when she got home
it was december
and the air
was black
cold. she was hard
and sharp, my sister;
brittle, you could say.
heartbroken, and cracking
only at the changing heat
like a glass
full of boiling
water.

D.S. Maolalai
Dublin, Ireland

On Becoming a Harp

1.
There have been many casualties,
martyrs too,
though they serve no purpose here. To be clear:

This is not a victim's poem.

2.
In an obvious dream
my bones grew light and long,
and like a song, I was a swan,

swimming, until seized.

In hands I could not see,
my neck splayed, wrecked
—drawn taut.
I was plucked,
        strung up
        into a harp.

Curious,
I didn't scream,
—I watched my feathers
                drift
until I woke,
        furious.

3.
A tambourine to the skull
has a particular ring,
so you are sure
you won't want to hear the song again.

But you don't leave,

and you're afraid
    that means you like it,
though you know

  —you *know*
 —you don't.

4.
Finally,
You unfreeze.
You let go

he
falls
down
the
long,
sad
well.

you hear the echoes
and you fear
   someday

   you might crave the brash notes,
his touch.

Joy S. Mahar
Redford, Michigan

To Be Daphne

Thighs press into
sturdy laurel
arms lifted
in eternal praise
of the sky

Returned to the cycle
of the Mother
toes dug into
her tender flesh
solid, steady
resistant

until he comes
softly in the dusk
she melts back
into pliable flesh
in his arms
sap quickens into
blood once more
racing into a
beating heart

Kristina Heflin
Albertville, Alabama

The Fox

The owners will be coming soon.
They left us keys to turn the locks.
Booted through their silent rooms,
we start the furnace, draw shades back.

The house blinks on her blanket
lawn, hungry for possession.

We fix the fence and watch a fox
circle round some stones—
a nest where little rabbits twine,
smelling warm and stunned.

Reverberant beneath the rocks
the sledge might sound like shots.
The fox in gray dust digging
finds the entrance that he sought—.

Even now, the owners drive
through fragments of Nebraska
they can't remember: shivering
grass, rest-stop trashcans.

Their eyes fixed to the border
line, always in recession.

Wind arrives; swings a window
to pass inside the house
and though we hammer late tonight,
it never comes back out.

Christian Woodard
Laramie, Wyoming

Telephone of the Wind

"Hello? Are you there? Can you hear me?"

The glass telephone booth sits on a hill
overlooking the Pacific Ocean.
The ocean, once my friend, is now my enemy
since the tsunami took Mimori away.

"Mimori, how are you? I am getting along. The
tomatoes you planted are ripe now.
I keep your bird feeder full. Our house
is being rebuilt, just as it was."

I'd dialed Mimori's number on the rotary phone.
I felt foolish at first,
it is not connected to anything.
But many people in Otsuchi
get answers here.

When I speak into the phone,
my voice sounds
like a lost bird flying high on the wind,
I repeat her name:
"Mimori,
Mimori,
Mimori."

I listen.
All I hear is the wind rushing up the hill
from the ocean.
It whispers
as it circles the booth
like an embrace.

Suzanne O'Connell
Los Angeles, California

What You Hold at Bay

Autumn, your faded brown capris
washed, tucked in a drawer.
You wonder if you'll be around
to wear them again next summer.
You're not limping into your late eighties
or living with Stage IV cancer,
only aware of how life can tilt toward
disaster at a doctor's phone call,
how crushed the red car you saw yesterday
on the highway appeared. How crazily
your president rants on television and Twitter,
how last winter you never had winter,
only the warmth of an extended autumn,
Gray's peepers singing from leafless trees,
except for one Arctic three-day weekend
when it snowed.

    And sometimes
sorrow flies up inside you
like a sparrow trapped in a wall,
thrashes until you fear
one day it will burst through.

Pam Baggett
Cedar Grove, North Carolina

On Her Blindness

I don't remember being aware at age four
that Mother was losing her eyesight;
my attention was captured by the grasshopper
I held prisoner in a Mason jar who kept eyes
upon escape when I inserted fresh grass;
by the bubble-eyed tadpoles I had scooped
from the creek and placed in a fish bowl;
and by how strange my name sounded when I
said it aloud with eyes closed; but I
sometimes cried on moonless nights
when darkness consumed my room.
She would come to my side and whisper,
"Don't be afraid. There's no reason to fear
the dark," but I would not be comforted.

Phillip Howerton
West Plain, Missouri

Coming Down in Changzhou

Every morning
the van arrives to take us
to the teacher's college.

We five Americans stand
behind the vehicle and push,
while the driver wakes the engine.

Most of our students
are young, recently arrived
from the western provinces—they want
to know not English, but how
to teach it. I learn the characters
for please, thank you, exit.

Dinner at our Hilton
buffet. My roommate
calls home to Indiana, daughter
and divorcing wife.

Before dawn, thirty stories
dreaming Jiangsu smog.

    We wake to sirens,
and the doomed high-rise shell
across the six-lane
shudders, sinks.

Stand at the window,
thighs chilled in industrial
air conditioning. Mortar dust,
blank stare of streetlamps,
bladder boiling.

                        James A. Miller
                        Baytown, Texas

The Mist Blower

Working in an office cubicle that he would prefer not to
in Brooklyn, Elijah is thankful for the mist blower
from across a rolling ocean under which a pipe lies
next to the telephone cables and the fiber optic cords
amongst the grossly translucent creatures feeding off
the volcanic energy from fissures in the ocean floor.
Elijah is grateful for the mist blower whose breath
he knows from its rhythm, from the billows in
the wall of mist that keeps him sane, if unpopular,
on the 41st floor. The mist blower is prone,
cherubic lips upon a copper tube that draws
the finest, grayest moisture from the air above
the peaks. The mist blower keeps Eastern Time
the better to write in the mornings in Derbyshire.
Far from a sinecure, the mist blower aches in
intercostal muscles but knows a wall of mist
trumpets a withdrawal in New York, a living with
beauty in clock time and in office cubicles.

Eleanor Reeds
Hastings, Nebraska

will no one love you Margaret

how the air bends
itself—her waist,
an acute appraisal
supplanting heat. geese
honk longing into reality, and the sugar maple
spurts. rustling the chandelier
grass-wicks
aflame, thrushes smoke themselves
out of church into the eaves,
where one may see
clouds centralize about your eye.
the sky moves gray, gray, gray,
see? geese's arrow-pointed brow
pierces Day into winter morsels.
a child's fist opens
on the accident of a crushed moth.
ash dapples earth: the glare of
having lived long without
light, where Time suspends
like a neck to observe
the grass bend

and wail.

Emily Ellison
San Marcos, Texas

Adulthood

Side by side in the cool grass
we look for Jupiter next to Orion.

I need to tell you something,
you say—reaching for my hand.

Sounds of ice cubes in glasses
the laughter of parents
drift across the lawn
where we hide in the shadows.

Anne's pregnant,
you say.
I mean, we are—it's mine.

A flock of birds rises
their noisy indignation
a reminder of our kisses
    child's play.

My mouth turns to sand.
My cheeks burn.
So you were lovers like that?
How did I miss the signs?

It's a trap.
It won't last.
It's already over.

I know this like I know
the river that runs through me,
its current strong and steady.

One day I will be everything.

Diana Donovan
Mill Valley, California

pawnee poem

here by the platte river where
the horizon teases us
with its nightly striptease
of golden sunbeams
swallowed by the red
shadows of sandhills
here scattered among
the sage and thistle lies
volumes of pawnee poems

here are scores of stanzas,
octaves, sestets, couplets calcified
and rotting like images in
modernist verse

here among the tufts of
bluestem are mostly bones
of buffalo but plenty bones
belong to pawnee

a jackknife picks these bones
clean and careful work
articulates them joint by joint
making of such bones
a song

Henry Krusiewicz
Fremont, Nebraska

Attendance

All the mornings like burnt offerings,
raising smoke to entice fickle deities
but mainly wasting what a child
could not do without. All my charges
dreaded numbered days, I kept pleasant
count. Especially in the testing rooms,
tucking laptops into sleepy carts,
I saw how futility usually dressed,
how any welcome is forgiveness
in a bad room, to never sit
if you want peace. Between lessons,

we traveled on the calendar, paid airlines
twice to do so. The sands were everything
we needed them to be. Then, we charted
nothing. We attended to the speeches
of our children. Between the months,
they grew, seismic. My love & I aged
into a calm, the kind no one calls
romantic, but peace is a transcendence
that isn't told, as much as escapes
a record that tallies only absence.

                                            Max Heinegg
                                   Medford, Massachusetts

Describe the Rain as Dishwater

as it falls from the shredded, worn
and wrung out rags of clouds rendered
as colorless as fog, and you
describe my day: the streets damp
yet grimy, the leaves of trees have
lost their green, the trunks drip gently
into the depths of their own shadows.
The daffodils droop in hang-dog
expressions along the walk. What
spark of sunshine lurking in that
washed-out yellow I cannot pry
out. My clothes are dull, if not gray,
on days like these, and I roll up
my sleeves to keep the damp away.

Deborah H. Doolittle
Jacksonville, North Carolina

The Old Woman Thinks the Doll Alive

She feeds and comforts her,
changes her diapers, hums a lullaby.

In rare lucid moments, she knows
    the doll is not real—*See,*
        her face is plastic, not skin.

The daughter marvels at such tenderness,
a quality not seen before,

believes a flood of blood swept away,
    not just her mother's mind,
        but the meanness too.

Wanting to believe the goodness
was there—hidden—all along.

Of little faith, I fear the old woman
    may yet revert—hurl her doll
        out the window.

I can see it floating in the nearby lake,
one leg broken off. No matter.

Daughters of fish drape sodden
    reeds on the doll's bald head,
        strands of hair afloat,

and occasionally, nibble at
the mermaid's tail, her fingers.

                          Vicki Mandell-King
                          Louisville, Colorado

The Man Who Worked for Me

He left every morning before
light came, while I slept blind
in the room he built for me.

At four-fifteen each afternoon
the every-damned-day dinner bucket
banging on his leg beat out
the steps he'd saved for reaching home.
His hard, sweet smell
rolled up the porch:
cutting oil in workshoe leather,
gabardine and splintered steel.

Soon, in the chair
with its back to the window,
the day's beer warming
in a bandaged hand,
he dozed.

Four thousand times I rattled by?
I broke his sleep with few hellos.
He woke to just the noise of me,
head coming up from workshirt chest
where he kept the daily smile.

Now the man who began my life
works at staying alive.
I bring him my son at twenty,
my daughter halfway to woman,
and what I've come to be.

He smiles at us, says it was worth
the work. That he sees his hand
in them. And me.

James Longstaff
Cazenovia, New York

Sun splashed rye grass, near rose perfume in the garden

I wish to catch it before I light
    the fire under the crisp-leaved-collards
        and the coldwater-filled kettle

the taste of frying shrimp
    on the long-ago river where Uncle
        fried catfish and hush puppies

when the Winnebago pulled up with my cousin
    stepping out in her blue blouse and tight
        black pants wearing our days together

with all the stories, the gone-away wisdom people
    now filling our arms, as we race
        toward one another ready to give them life

the farm, the mule, the althea tree—
    that life, backlit and obsolete, full
        of contradiction, what we chose to remember

Libby Bernardin
Georgetown, South Carolina

Of Snow

A quick look around. I see a neighbor,
Eager to put out her red wicker chair,
Rest in the root system of early spring.

Would that I could be content, count
Petal after petal falling into my hand.
I prefer the cold, the huddle of bodies

At the bus stop, each of us waiting
For the white-out of a neap evening,
Our lives to be made all over again,

Layer upon layer of snow on our skin.
Till shivering, we empty out our souls,
Find in the small heap, the evening star,

The light sufficient to make our way
Through the city, glad we have not
Scattered or worst, falling, disappear.

Mary Ann Meade
Lansdowne, Pennsylvania

June,

This poem is written in response to "Poem About My Rights" by June Jordan.

I'm afraid to walk alone at night but I am not afraid
of solitude
the swaying leaves
don't incite fear in me/ leave me be/ don't leave me
chin pressed shoulders but not broken
limb that tries falling on top of me and what if it succeeds
is it really one in three but like you I need
to be alone tonight too I feel like night belongs
belongs to me but was it stolen/ swallowed
whole by a van with no windows and
spit out in the corner of a room with no windows
vein syringed in a different
city in a different state
by a different name it's been
pushed
pushed and penetrated like you
tell about Namibia and Angola and Zimbabwe it's been
pinned
down by colonizing eyes
it can feel
the voyeuristic invasion prying its thighs
biding time for the sun
biding time it can feel—
June—
I used to walk alone at night
drunk or high forgetting about/ recalling about what the night
used to feel like/ about but then there was that one/ number of/
    statistic of
times catcalls chasing me and me
pretending not to see
the words
reaching creeping thrusting
at me the dog whistles turned
bitch and *look at me* and now
when I walk alone at night I can only see

the thieves the hungry vans the eyes of trees the hisses
dehumanizing me the time Frank closed his arm/ my throat and
 away
partially pocketed the night and before
that it was my father and before that it was my father's hand
 clapping
rhythm on my rosy cheeks and the tug of war
of the gallon of milk and the plate of spaghetti on my sister's face
 and
my brother's football injuries and my oldest sister's nails
her nails digging
as I stood between
her and her ability to leave and all the women I know
inside or outside at night
it used to belong to us, June—the moon
and the stars and our youths—promised to us, June—
but I know
like you, I need
the night
it belongs to me it cries
but cannot be sympathized June
what am I or you but a woman alone at night
a woman the night
even now June even now

Calida Osti
West Lafayette, Indiana

Melancholy

I can't help but love her
When she comes,
Carrying a black blanket
And the bones of my lost children.
We dive under
The soft dark water
And hold our breath.
The moon stops waxing,
Holds her sharp crescent
Ready.

But then the sun rises,
And the lizards come out
To soak in the heat
And to hunt.
The light distorts her,
And she struggles
To keep me under.
She wants me like I've always been,
Submissive, immobile, protected.

She draws me close
Until all I can see
Are the endless days coming
Like blood seeping through the bandages,
And movement seems impossible, unnecessary.
We draw slow breaths together,
Counting the cockroach shells
On the kitchen shelves,
Accumulating layers of cat hair and dust
In the stillness of our grief.
She wraps my hair in her hands and hums
A song from when we were young,
when we'd hide in the corn fields
and wait all day to be missed.

Roxanne Prillwitz
Tucson, Arizona

Local Giraffe

I'm too tall to buy lottery tickets
and a chocolate doughnut
at 7-11. However,

I have good conversations
with the water tower. I'm up high
so we can chat.
It's hard to be a water tower.
You attract lightning. Kids climb you.
When you pray, you can't get down
on your knees. Still, you keep
your head in the clouds, or near them,
so you dream sweetly.

My neighbor Peg calls me exotic.
She's the exotic one, singing
"Oh Promise Me" to windy laundry.
When someone buys a new car,
people say, "Congratulations!"
It's like an award. I can't fit in
a car. My legs find their way
to wherever I care to go. I may

leave someday. The city
looks exciting. The country does too.
I'm preparing many lives.

Kenneth Pobo
Media, Pennsylvania

Trespass

You've seen the signs,
POSTED on so many premises:
you and your footprint are

not welcome. Yet what can
there be to fear in this wide
Christian corridor where

you are surrounded
by huggers of scripture,
where weekly they urge

their compliant Almighty
to follow their good example
and forgive them their trespasses?

Mark Metcalf
Sutton, Nebraska

The Poet Parents

Never one to see much past the next
necessary word, he found himself
unprepared for the consequences of
falling in love with the novelist.

Her idea of life, full, complicated,
intensely textured, populated with
storied characters and re-emerging
themes, crowded his illusion of
control and the contemplative life.

While he'd kept his extended family
at a comfortable distance, her people
infiltrated his life; once joined to one
of theirs, actual blood ties meant no
more than legal commitments.

Terrified by the mere thought of
infants and children, he nevertheless
found himself relieved when the
novelist's belly began to swell,
because the in-laws stopped asking
to see his poems.

Charissa Menefee
Ames, Iowa

Walking on Broughton & Hillsborough

I crush a fresh french fry as I walk the street
and I remember the nights I was hungry
    empty but couldn't eat
    tired but couldn't sleep

The bustling, boisterous street was too buoyant
the security guards around all focused and waiting
for my eyelids to shut

Honestly, I was full
High off the egg roll steam stabbing through inch-thick glass
wondering how in God's name I wasn't hungry

I threw myself away that week
prayed for friends to find warmth in bed
Most aren't friends any longer

In the mornings, I washed up in the gym
I wore a blue raincoat even as the humid heat grew
thank God my backpack was stronger

The ant I saw stumbling over french fries was God,
reminding me I'd never be bigger than He
I pitied the ant as it fell into cheese while
I stepped over and walked free

Patricia Lauren Ndombe
Knightdale, North Carolina

Into the Woods

Under a tarp strung clear across dewy,
heavy air, we sleep communal
on crackling plastic in the dark acres
behind the lake. There is singing

by guitar and spider hunt by flashlight
held to the forehead, a way to leave
the fire and hold hands with someone
a few charged moments. Then back,

no secrets showing. We think it's chance
the way the cabins are paired, this boys'
with that girls', and not the counselors' design,
who together sleep by the fire, away

from their charges. In the first quiet
of lying down, some girl tells the story:
entire camping groups missing in the woods,
or maybe one girl at a time, maybe only

those who strayed alone too far into the trees.
The last ones to fall asleep hear a carnival
of sound, amplified with every cracking twig,
every rhythm that must, we think, be footfalls.

Daddy-Long-Legs tickles us like night's fingers.
Soon, someone wakes with a kick, sits up, touched
on her face or hair. We're 12, 13, 14.
We hear something's there before we can name it.

Jennifer Brown
Raleigh, North Carolina

Angel of Repose

Between remnants
of Sunday sermons
and my conscience,
your voice is audible
    like the creak
    of a door that moves
    when the wind blows.

Brushstrokes of mauve
watch from my ceiling
    when on Mondays I share my bed
    with a man. He puts roses
    on my pillow. I feel his breath
    on my face,
yet your whispers
from behind pillars
distract.

I live in a world
    of skittish winds
    and shifting hands
a world
    of wildfires and neon lights,
    and my cat has fleas. In the dark
your halo shines,
a crescent moon lopsided.

    Today my phone rings,
    my faucet drips and drips,

but then during the night
    when the Ghost Ship burned
    to the ground, when 36 charred bodies
    were carried out.
there was your deadly silence.

As a child I used to lie on the ground
brushing wings onto the melting snow.

Tonight I crave the flight
of ravens.

Angelika Quirk
San Rafael, California

Burial

After Christine Gosnay

Then was the day I came into your bed, lay down
and began to bleed a stain
onto your pillowtop mattress.
Your hands held over me, ancient stone fingers
and your leaden palms.

Then we felt despair,
aching like a deep breath with a broken rib.

The snowdrifts sealed us in,
there was no other world.

The wet winter had hardened
the trees' hearts against the earth
and matted their leaves under a forgiving sky.

You tried to speak to me,
and the ash blistering my knuckles
made it hard to look at you while I stiffened
under the grimy yellow street light.

Then the sky pleaded for a dark morning.
Then no more hearts to bleed shapes in your bed.
You would not let me leave, two halves
in the dark January. I left you

in the snowplow ice mounds
and you waited, and you waited.

Olivia Swasey
Brighton, Massachusetts

Barnacle

Black coffee and the wind picks up.
In the harbor, boats—moorings loosed
from the bottom sand—pitch—

stuttered rise and fall, frantic salt water—
it is in the air.
A dingy batters the rocks, batters to splinters.

Wind shaking the house now—
a storm comes through.
Screen door wails—broken
hinges—thrashes the vinyl siding.

Candles in the windows—
there is still power, but I know.
The neighbor's trees are unsteady.

The coffee spills onto the counter,
spools around a pot—
dried marram grass
moving in drafts through old walls.

No dish rags in the drawer.
Outside,
terns diving, unimpaired
toward the rocks, rolling
like kids' marbles
on the shore.

Casey Lynn Roland
Beverly, Massachusetts

Notes from the Dragon's Autopsy

We tried to remove the bulky yellow eyes first
but they crumbled at our touch
like sunflowers dipped in liquid helium

Slashed open the throat with a whale scythe—
nothing but a lining of charred tissues
nothing we couldn't contain

Heart: a seemingly
well-gummed nugget
of iron pyrite

A gray, grizzled sky

Hacked open the stubborn skull
and hopped right in!
No brain, but the space smelled like darkroom chemicals
the air leered in red light
the walls seemed to be dreaming us:
exact exposures of the Dickens boy, laboring
In his blacking factory

No foliage on the looming trees, but wind
riffling the brittle blue scales
makes the sound of English rain
or rustling leaves

Finally cut to a place that hissed
and saw where all the blood had pooled

We dunked our beakers, drank, and wept

We slept under the
torn tents of the wings

Scott Thomas Lumbard
Tucson, Arizona

Objects of Shame

Kurt—the hard, chalky cheese—
has to be softened by saliva, by the breath
before it can be consumed.

Hidden sinewy bodies,
in a Gulag camp for women
outside Astana,
thrashed in terror
under a black mustache.

Starving women working on the steppe,
the guards watching nearby
and local villagers looking
through the gates, grimacing,
pelting the imprisoned women with stones.

Picking those rocks from the ground,
the women found these were not
objects of shame, but hardened Kurt—
small, hand-rolled balls of dried dairy,
reserve food, offered by their enemies.

Extra flesh to aid
women in motionless winter.

Alyssa Ross
Auburn, Alabama

The Least I Can Do

She held her finger in front of me—
5 stitches she said,
5 stitches to fix the damage of one knife hidden at the bottom
of a sink of sudsy water

I did not turn my eyes away as I once would have,
no fear today of her scar,
no belief that her life would be much altered

for when you can see the scar,
5 stitches or 50,
you know what damage has been done

To know is to accept—at least at some level—
that she will heal

I will not turn away;
It's the least I can do to validate another's hurt

It's the least I can do

Becky Faber
Lincoln, Nebraska

At the carne asada

My mother tells our family that I want
to be a writer. They ask if I'm gay.
She tells them no. She tilts her chin
to the sun and says, *he writes poetry.*
The air quiets and the grass stands upright.
The women line their faces with grins,
what great chisme this will be, they think.
And to everyone's surprise, the men
stop drinking. *Read them something,*
she says. I swirl my near-empty coke can
and stare at my feet. She runs to the car,
grabs my journal and reads,
skin is just a poor excuse for a prison.
There is a deep silence and then laughter.
They call me 'little convict' and ask
me for stories from the inside.
We eat our carne asada at home now.

Gabriel Mundo
Highwood, Illinois

The War Started. A Cartoon

The war started. A cartoon
elephant graced the screen.
Earlier, we pretended dying
in the street. We collapsed
onto dinner later. On TV
the characters laughed.
We laughed too. Much
was made of how much
more food the elephant ate
than was expected.
We were full. Of news
we had had enough.
So when the anchors broke
their eyes, falling left
to right, but to us
stumbling right to left,
we declared the animation
better than dessert,
retiring to rehearse
tomorrow's protest.

Thomas Mixon
Sunapee, New Hampshire

A Ballad of Anchors & Scythes

Wind's the same but not the music.
Enough time, alone, & no language
has a chance to bring a lover back,
or confuse longing for anything
other than what it has
always been: loss. Gulls, for hours,

insist no violin, no matter how supple
the wrist holding the bow, has a prayer
of touching the sordid
sliver of moon that slices clouds
dusk till dawn. It's indifference, the gulls
bark in their best sea voices, that tears

lovers apart. Knowing no one is
coming to lure the moon back
to its old notions of romance,
the wind & gulls & what light there is
compose a hymn no woman would
hum, a music to anchor the moon.

George Looney
Erie, Pennsylvania

Lights Out

The café light blinks "OPEN," but it ain't welcoming no more:
You can't reclaim the days of idle chatter,
with/all/the cluttered thoughts or the relentless texts
banging/left at the chime decorated door.

You can't reclaim the days of idle chatter
amidst the dirty dishes piled high
and left at the chime decorated door
awaiting line cooks that are no more.

Amidst the dirty dishes piled high,
delivery trucks rumble, dishes shatter, a ceramic chip drops,
awaiting line cooks that are no more
along with forgotten newspaper *dailies* stacked in the corner.

Delivery trucks rumble, dishes shatter, a ceramic chip drops,
haunting aluminum chairs and square-shaped tables
along with forgotten newspaper dailies stacked in the corner,
packed away, leaving a sidewalk bare.

Haunted aluminum chairs and square-shaped tables
making way for all that's shiny and grand.
Now packed away, leaving a sidewalk bare
with wider walkways: More bodies, less touch.

Making way for all that's shiny and grand,
confused regulars look up, then around, for answers.
With wider walkways: More bodies, less touch,
peak through dusty windows, catching tiny *glimpses* of lipstick-
    stained mugs.

Confused regulars look up, then around, for answers.
Graffiti filled table tops, heavily etched with initials of lives past,
peak through dusty windows, catching tiny *reflections* of lipstick-
    stained mugs
and white chalk still visible on the now mostly faded blackboard.

Graffiti filled table tops, heavily etched with initials of lives past,
settle in the darkness and dust, as a tiny mouse scampers,

anticipating the broom and shriek that no longer follow
and white chalk still visible on the now mostly faded blackboard.

The café light blinks "OPEN," but it ain't welcoming no more.

Jen Schneider
Dresher, Pennsylvania

Night Light

Photinus pyralis
(Big Dipper firefly)

in the gloam
flotsam from upriver
errant flip-flops, pocked styrofoam
beer bottle shards, weary tires
nuzzled by stale brown froth
vanish in sips of shadow.
a fire beetle flashes lambent semaphore
feisty clarion for the Manichaean struggle
at the signal, cicadas drill
raspy tinnitus into aching brains
blue-bellied frogs eruct in loud growls
mosquitoes rail at that good night
vaulted sky blackens.
another burst of the blinking green
tick of the glow-fly's digital clock
swamp iris and muskroot whisper fresh scents
gobbets of rotten spoonbill cats
shout coarse odor of decay
the void yawns.
above the backwater armada
retinue of plastic cups and mutilated garments
one more salvo of pulsing flame
the lightning bug's parting effort to stitch
earth's warm, lush muck
to the nothing of sky
then vacant dark.

E. R. Lutken
Saint Joseph, Louisiana

dead language

cave-wall creatures
iron oxide and ochre, rock against rock
lapis lazuli ground with care
in that stone there

this is a lost voice
unsilenced
relic words preserved here
bard-weavings
retold between friends
lions without teeth
bulls without legs
hands severed at the wrist

songs so precious once
hidden within caves
from side-eye questions and
mouths with jagged tongues
lost to collective judgment
import sealed in stone
divination alone

as it was in the beginning

what this poet must have carried
to keep writing
stories bastard-born
no circle of huts could bear to hear
nothing comes out in a straight line

the animals run on for miles

Debora Ewing
Annandale, Virginia

Yeghegnadzor: Arid Orange

A plump pearl belly, she cups the spider in a wine glass,
lets out onto the porch in a canopy of hornbeam
an eight-legged escape onto a spaded leaf, along arms,
over elbows, down a body of mossy bark to blend
its back into rain mud, into a pool between roots,
into strands tall enough to hide snakes and other creatures
that move clandestine to watchers with empty stomachs,
that sense the seasons through cool and warm soils,
through pound of spade, flood of storm, frozen earth
when suns drop behind the horizon a little longer.

Alex Vartan Gubbins
West Bend, Wisconsin

Ode to a Centipede

This time I am ready for you—
albeit tentatively.
I no longer shriek

at the sight of you
scuttling across the floor,
swift and silent,

looking like a mustache
frantically searching
for a naked upper lip.

In the silence of the night,
you freeze on the tiled wall
when I flick on the bathroom light.

We stare at each other,
or whatever it is you do with those
wispy antennae that sense my presence.

No longer enemies,
I see you now as a visiting artist,
appreciating your choreography

as if you were all 36 Rockettes
gliding across the floor
in perfectly synchronized motion.

Gloria Heffernan
Syracuse, New York

Why Are All of the White Babies at the Deep End of the Swimming Pool?

White people throw small babies into eight feet of water with reckless abandon

And as they are about to be tossed into this possibility of a watery grave,
these children
giggle

And once they are flung into the unknown abyss
they sink,
and seconds later emerge from the deep
and float

Just like that
white. babies. float.

Their heads are effortlessly above water
smiling at the bright sun

Meanwhile, there is a group of black children
cowering in the corner of the shallow end of the pool

crying

shivering

cloaked with fear

my four year old son is among them

I look at the smiling white baby
I look at my son
I look back at the smiling white baby,
and I make a decision

my son will float

In a world designed to sink little black boys to the bottom of the pool
as if their spirits were made of bricks,

I decided, my son will float

I slowly approach him and guided him to the deep end of the pool
I want him to splash and smile at the sunshine like the white babies
I lift him to the sky,
and just as I am about to hurl him in
he looks into my eyes with sadness

He speaks to me with those eyes, not his voice
"There is a reason I'm afraid of the water, mama."
"It's in my DNA."

And in that moment, I understand.
black babies know what that water represents
it is the Middle Passage
the voyage across the Atlantic into centuries of bondage

Black babies don't emerge from the water happy and swimming
they emerge traumatized
with fear that the vast ocean of the swimming pool will drown
    them,
and if they should be unlucky enough to survive
that journey to the middle of the deep end,
they will endure the bondage that completing the passage means

So, with great sadness, I lower him
and let him run back down the heated concrete
and walk down three stairs,
only to stand in the shallow end with the other black babies

he will not rise to the top today

he will not float

He will watch the joy on the white babies' faces
as they rise to the top
as they swim
as they survive the deep end

Monica Weatherly
Lithia Springs, Georgia

Once Upon a Time, There Were Two Girls

in the suburbs. One was a half-
girl and the other whole.

Through the woods,
they shimmered, telling stories

that glimmered
like the oil-slicked creek.

    In the beginning,
            they said,

*The crabapple birthed
a baby girl*

    or *The story goes
Lilith molded from the red*

*clay earth then Eve wrenched
from Adam's rib.*

        They laughed
and they laughed. There,

no bear or blackberry,
just bramble. They believed

mothers plucked babies
from trees, wondered

if they'd ever want
for a man, even a kind one

cursed. How could there be
such thing as *happily*

       ever after
when after all, all girls

have been swayed
by a forked tongue, held

captive as a crown?

Stacey Balkun
New Orleans, Louisiana

Running from December

I wake early and reach to find
your empty pillow on your empty side
of the bed. Is this how it will be, I think
if you were to die before me?

Our old mutt is stirring,
his tail thumping against the painted wall.
You always thought his yawn was fascinating,
his mottled tongue, the yellowed carnassials,
betray his age.

Now, the furnace clicking on,
the rush of hot air from out of the pipes.
And our children have left their beds.
I can hear their quick, eager footsteps down the hall,
the wooden floors warp and groan.

Soon, they will be knocking on, pushing open
our bedroom door, crying
for food like little birds. Soon,
the snow will fall in wet lacy ribbons again,
amongst the last of the flowers
you planted once, like a child,
so delicately, so lovingly in the yard.

Brett Thompson
Gilmanton, New Hampshire

Firewood

The eldest daughter prefers to weedeat,
and thus lays down the lawn law every weekend.

Eager to please, the youngest sibling
picks up dead oak limbs and highway trash
of Pall Mall packs, Bud cans, and Sonic cups.

Others mow, trim hedges, upright the bird bath
and gargoyles their stepfather bats
like fastballs he once conquered in high school—
now he's a cliché and brags Springsteen
wrote "Glory Days" in his honor.

And the oldest knows that song
as deeply as the sharp blade of the moon
when it pitches down through the forest
in November. When the electricity is gone,

the slip of a ghost, not returning
anytime soon. So she gathers the little ones
like acorns, shovels them into her bed,
stacks them up for warmth like firewood.

Dave Malone
West Plains, Missouri

How to Pan for Gold

Don't look in the dog's mouth,
no precious metals cap those teeth.
And slobber isn't the same as a river,
spittle doesn't lead to a stream.

Wander outside and breathe the air.
Some people detect what may glitter
from a great distance, many feet
or yards or lawns, before any river.

You need patience and caution
to surmise natural alchemic endeavor,
stirring the iron of our hard hearts
flooded with all our blood's copper.

After rain, sediment could contain
flecks, dislodged or even peened.
So much sloshing and staring at
sand in your pan, specks to be seen.

Your hands must get dirtier
for the ground to duly nourish.
False hope comes day after day.
Even pyrite offers middling flourish.

Ronnie Sirmans
Lawrenceville, Georgia

The Mask

In dark and somnolent
churches, a giggle
goes infectious.
Serious citizens
study their toes or
the rafters
as the preacher
piques. Studies
show the miserable
who smile grow
happy in a short
while. It's better
than food. Even
the bawling baby
proselytizing in
the grocery aisle
responds to a grin
despite the mood
he's in. For old men
too, in the end,
the mask becomes
the true.

P M F Johnson
Minneapolis, Minnesota

Something to Write Home About

The brain doesn't care who is coming and going, the
seasons where tone is a voice in a parallel universe,

or that particular moment when Dad believed he could
survive as a stick figure among the hungry. In time,

the street people disappeared, but not before the
members of their glee club joined the secret march to

Magic City, and the lights in the cavern blew themselves
out. Noted for its unexpected forays into turbulence,

the quick fix was unlocked, and the radical fan boys
brought up through the ranks of soundless tundra,

the various subspecies arranged in hairline fractures,
a wall of subtext separating my favorite comic books

from do-it-yourself, jerk-the-penguin, railroad funnies.
Things too unreal to be from western New York,

a note of panic in the whispering village.

Michael Malan
Corvallis, Oregon

Volcano

I remember when you lived with us,
your easy smile, the missing teeth concealed,
your blond hair and giant, gentle hands.
You spread out from a chair as if still growing
even though you were thirty
and all your growing was done.

You'd come home laughing.
I was only a little bit bad, you said.
Held up by the wall
until you slid down to the floor in the laundry room.
I tried to kick you out
but you gave me a roll of hot, sweaty bills, and that was that.

We lived that way for some time,
mashed potatoes and ground beef,
curry made you sick, the smell of it.
You'd come home laughing,
but then you'd come home shaking
and need gas money so you could go to work.

Our pretty balcony
in the sunshine, the view
gradually obscured by beer cans, the drain clogged by butts
until it became a puddle of misery on the second floor.
You had to go, but you had no place to go.
We stood for a while, unmoving.

I remember when you lived with us,
your wide mouth, your soft hair and strong body,
you poured out on the chair like molten lava,
a smoking, drinking volcano,
but you eroded,
and finally washed away.

Celia Meade
Salt Spring Island, British Columbia, Canada

Hard-bitten Body

Even the quality of pain
is disinterested:
dull, nagging, intermittent.
The knees' percussive crepitus,
muscles cross. Ecstasy
is equivocal or a myth.
It's more like satisfaction
in the first coffee,
a bowel movement,
a laugh.

The body's receptors are
unimpressed.
It takes more of something
to feel a charge: perhaps
a brush with death,
a shock to reset the soul,
that fraction of a second
in a lightning storm
that illuminates what is
and then subtracts it,
a moment of binary vision
to blast the slumber
of slow loss.

Andrea Fry
New York, New York

Surrender

Even in the dark this autumn evening,
as we two lie on our bellies under a juniper tree,
they keep barking through the underbrush.

The spruce and maples try to shield us,
but in the dusk they've picked up our scent,
harmless boys playing a game,
posing as spies in an alien land.

In the dusk of an autumn evening
cocker spaniels turn into snarling hounds.

Heart pounding. Breath deafening.
A man and woman, half hidden
by shriveling leaves, hold their leashes.

We throw ourselves on their mercy.

Victor Altshul
New Haven, Connecticut

Dry

Clotheslines are banned
from these yards. A certain tone
is being sought, and it fails
to include anything old or poor,
anything that reveals a lack
of taste, or a ragged surplus
of the plain or bare, of flapping secrets.

I suggested that they mistake
sheets for shrouds
and old shirts for bandages,
that they are afraid some stains
will not dissolve, that fading table linen
might say something they don't want to hear,
but I was voted down.

Our common laundry
will not have the right or freedom
to snap in the afternoon's bright wind.
We'll have no tenement alleys
hung with foreign flags,
no doubtful families of underclothes
bickering over who gets what.

Our motto on these streets
is *Take it Inside*,
and everyone will have to live by that,
every smelly heap, each rude unfolding,
working out its own sanitation
in a private place, while sunlight
by the basketful goes unwanted.

Monty Jones
Austin, Texas

Moving Day

Clock hands deliberate, a slow turning,
    stars ascending, descending;
the Pleiades depart, no longer
conjunct. In the yard I walk

where a weeping cherry
    strewed petals and chocolate
labs performed mock battles
among territory we no longer

possess, ceded to another. The grill
flaked with rust, abandoned in the
    summer light. A heap of
cardboard boxes piled on the street.

I watch your car pull out of the
    driveway; loaded heavily, it sinks,
mattress swaying on the roof. A long
summer knitted us together,

now events rupture that clarity,
and the air hums with the
unspoken. Imagined children
    scatter like dust in the wind.

Claudia Buckholts
Somerville, Massachusetts

The Coffee Table

The feast begins with coffee
and a few flakes from raisin toast,
a dawn of caffeine and sugar
to light the day.
Later come tasty remnants
of popcorn, hot cocoa,
sticky juices and tiny morsels
of secreted chocolate,

all to be graciously wiped away
by that diligent sweeper—
the dog's pernicious tongue,
though it can barely reach
the current accumulation
of cookie crumbs in each corner
where the glass surface
sits in wood.

Some hidden drops of ice cream
and various debris
decorate the area rug beneath,
too fancy for a play room
but no one minds,
any child is welcome
along with a smidgen of imagination
and his canine partner

to the table piled high
with Lego space stations
and elaborate ships
flown by fantastic creatures
through galaxies
beyond our own
in search of adventures
where good always prevails.

Georgette Unis
Claremont, California

Phone Conversations with an Outdated Insurance Claim

The key scrapes along the ridges
as if made for a different lock.

I left the window open and inside is cool with the night air.

I used to live where I used to live,
each successive addition to the end of a long list of imitation.

I turn the TV on, then off again.
Immediately regretting the attempt at normalcy.

What ever happened to Scott Bakula?

The bottle is lighter than I remember it.
Nighttime forays into forgiveness.

I don't know what day it is,
It might be yesterday.

The concrete around me,
cracks under the weight of winter.

My voice crackles from disuse
as I call to the window.

It might be yesterday I tell them.

They agree.

Devon Clements
Hastings, Nebraska

Pulling Down the Peach Tree, 1964

Lightning split the peach tree down
the middle and shook the house one night.
That weekend, bees attacked the peaches
that sat in the sun and rotted on the ground.
My brother Mark and I were afraid of bees.
Grandpa said, "The bees won't hurt you,"
as they covered the peaches with small coats
of stingers. My grandfather hooked a chain
around the bumper of his sea green 1952
Ford Crestline and the other end around one
section of the peach tree, then he yelled for dad
to "Go Ahead." The chain sprung to life
in the air and yanked against the chrome
bumper. The car coughed and dug up a patch
of grass then the tree gave way to a loud
crack and the white meat of the wood glowed
there in the broken wound. A great hole
in the lawn exposed roots and worms
and the deep life of the earth. Mark and I
stood in our chore overalls and waited
for Dad and Grandpa to shoo the bees away.

Michael Catherwood
Omaha, Nebraska

I Write to You

I write to you, a ghost, in the rain that is passing,
Sluicing the page with lost words and torn memories,
Rattling glass windows in wooden frames, while bared bone buds
Mock the story you no longer taste, hear or feel.

I will not be forgotten. Open the window. Touch me. I fall
Between sleeping and waking; wet, the yellow cab tires
Reverberate on the turtle-backed square cobblestones
Of Greene Street, awkward, uneven, windy, I am

The five-story tarp covering the scaffolding of your
So-called life. You cannot hide from me even in a city of windows,
Or a galaxy of walls and regret. I am water,
Facing death from another side of life.

I write: *Do not be afraid.* I write: *Taste what is falling,*
It will not be forgotten, not by you, not by me.
Together we can open the window of this poem,
Touch our past, present, and future, all to the beat of the rain

Syncopating on metal joists, rattling scaffolding, storied
Skeletons. I will relinquish my heart to your ears: you are me,
In this poem, a ghost, falling, dying, in the silence of the living.
This is our song: rejoice.

Evalyn Lee
London, England

Chamoy Lollypop

I've learned to love you is to take you whole—
the sour and the scald of you, the ruse
of candy on a stick, a glowing coal
that floods the mouth with spit. I could refuse
your sizzling, the prang and pang you bring,
but still I'll go in for another lick
and prove my lips can savor anything.
Beneath that rough exterior, a slick

of dulcet watermelon hides, the core
a tender startling of syrup sweet,
nectarous reward to soothe the sore
and tired tongue. I've learned to love this treat—
this lollypop of sugar and of fire
dissolved by my persistent mouth's desire.

Katherine Hoerth
Omaha, Nebraska

A Knack for Folding Things

The night before I left, Mother helped me pack.
Silently she ironed and folded, ironed
and folded. Lying face down on her bed
she cried. "Two years is so long,
You'll be so far away." I didn't understand,
I offered no comfort. I closed the door
then folded final pieces on my own,
trying to make edges crisp and flat like hers.
I packed and shut the suitcase trapping
all the words I hadn't yet learned how to say.

Mother returns, greeting me in dreams,
smiling and folding, arranging all my clothes
in silent rows, ready for some long journey.
It seems like spring, the lilacs in full bloom,
long before the stroke, the broken hip.
I tell her mothers have a knack for folding things,
a knack like many I'd learned from her.
As she melts into shadows, I try to bridge
that space between us, to hold the dream before
it dissolves. To pull it toward the light of day.

Kathleen Corcoran
Owings Mills, Maryland

Goodbye Earth,

The naked mole rat has no pain receptors on his skin. He adjusts his body to the temperature of unoxygenated underground, blinds himself to the darkness, binds himself to the dirt with his gnashing ground-grinded teeth. Digs into the belly of dark spinnings, tears into the maggot mud Technicolor, increasing velocity, into the core, until he comes exploding out wearing new ribbons in his hair, travels on rockets into salted space. Speeding ahead to dark and unpolluted landscapes.
And we see a lone taillight munching at the stars.

Melissa Sanders
Louisville, Kentucky

Cycle of Nature

A new twist perhaps on an old story—
my friend tells of the twenty ton humpback
beached on a Cape Cod shore, dead on arrival.
Carcass towed to Sandy Neck Beach where back-
hoes and trucks remove dismembered parts,
organs sent to Woods Hole for analysis, flippers,
other remains to be eaten by maggots, skeleton
to be assembled someplace in Maine. Down
the beach road he caught the waft of rotting flesh,
decay, watched gulls and crows eye the catch
of the day, swoop down, gobble what they can.
Cycle of nature many would say, but to me
what killed such a large animal so close to shore,
will we ever really know. My friend reminisces
in our animal sojourn on baby rabbits in his yard
he inadvertently stepped on beneath lavender,
blueberry bush. A sudden crack followed by
a squeal then shuddering as his foot fell.

Marc Swan
Freeport, Maine

Paper Lips

I remember telling myself one night—
I have a heart of clay, and stories that curdle like cheese—
I am knit together with wood and straw,
Occasionally set on fire.
My dreams dress themselves with sinew covering,
And I throw kisses like stones,
Tie constellations together on the rope of my thoughts and
Sling Orion like a bullet into the corridors of academic literature.
So, I spill myself into words and my words are drunk on shots of
    gin,
And I don't know if I ever told you, but
My soul is a smashed pear, sweet and ugly,
Hidden in the folds of a page.

But a still, small voice came to me and told me that
I am more arrogant than a
Baby pelican with a Heineken in its hand,
I've got a beak dripping with fish slipping like thoughts
Swallowed by the whales of words written in waves,
I want to stitch these fish into the waters and drown the slave that
    I am;
Wring these pages dry, so that I am dry.
I'm sick of stars, so I took a stiletto from my cynical hell
And cut a scar out of the forgotten corner of heaven,
Called it the moon and let it drip and bleed with its blue
And bruised glow—and while it started singing its sorrow,
I realized that I am no better than any, and much worse than most.

                                               Sara Lynn Burnett
                                                   Alpine, Texas

My Traveling Heart

I have traveled the universe,
From profound anguish
To immobilizing fear
To anger so hot the only place
I could live was my solitude.

Back home now,
My anger more a simmer than a boil—
Still fearful, but not often paralyzed,
Still bleeding,
I see that sorrow is forever,
But it is tempered with moments of quiet grace.

Friends stay close by
Even when my needle is stuck.
People who understand my wounded heart
Are wounded and perplexed with me

We thought we knew you,
Though you did not know yourself
How damaged you were by childhood's bruises—
Even love could not stop the bleeding.
Some wounds cannot be staunched.

Barbara Ryder-Levinson
Azusa, California

her heart upon her sleeve for daws to peck at

i see right through you, he'd said,
and she'd wondered what he meant:
she thought she was transparent.

nothing in her heart but on her face,
nothing on her face she did not mean.
her husband says her skin is alabaster
but she prefers to say she's made of glass.

now it occurs to her that glass is fragile,
that it can be smashed.

if love were as frail, as breakable,
as bodies, or reputation, or trust—
if it didn't cling stubbornly to life,
though you thought all the life crushed out of it

if it didn't revive when you least expected,
and speak soft lies where truth would cut,
she would have died unshriven and unstained,
but untruth clouds her over.

the shards of her were hungry for blood
so she tried to feed them with what she had:
Nobody. I myself.
Farewell.

Maya Chhabra
New York, New York

Trust your instincts.

Subscribe to *Plainsongs*.

Name: _____

Address: _____

_____

E-mail: _____

☐ One-year print subscription ($20)
☐ Two-year print subscription ($35)
☐ Three-year print subscription ($50)
☐ One-year e-subscription ($10)

Please send check and order form to:
　　　Plainsongs
　　　Hastings College
　　　710 Turner Ave.
　　　Hastings, NE 68901

CPSIA information can be obtained
at www.ICGtesting.com
Printed in the USA
BVHW071401140120
569037BV00003B/9/P

9 781942 885733